Samuel French Acting Edition

Milk Like Sugar

by Kirsten Greenidge

D0707276

‖SAMUEL FRENCH‖

ISBN 978-0-573-70036-1

www.concordtheatricals.com
www.concordtheatricals.co.uk

FOR PRODUCTION INQUIRIES

UNITED STATES AND CANADA
info@concordtheatricals.com
1-866-979-0447

UNITED KINGDOM AND EUROPE
licensing@concordtheatricals.co.uk
020-7054-7200

Each title is subject to availability from Concord Theatricals Corp.,
depending upon country of performance. Please be aware that *MILK
LIKE SUGAR* may not be licensed by Concord Theatricals Corp. in
your territory. Professional and amateur producers should contact the
nearest Concord Theatricals Corp. office or licensing partner to verify
availability.

This work is published by Samuel French, an imprint of Concord
Theatricals Corp.

MUSIC AND THIRD-PARTY MATERIALS USE NOTE

IMPORTANT BILLING AND CREDIT REQUIREMENTS

Originally commissioned and the World Premiere of *MILK LIKE SUGAR* produced by the La Jolla Playhouse, La Jolla, California (Christopher Ashley, Artistic Director & Steven Libman, Managing Director).

It was inspired by attendance at the Aspen Institute's Ideas Festival and was the recipient of Aspen Theatre Masters Visionary Playwright Award and commissioned by Theatre Masters (Julia Hansen, Artistic Director).

Playwrights Horizons, Inc., Women's Project Productions, and La Jolla Playhouse produced the New York City premiere of *MILK LIKE SUGAR* Off Broadway in 2011.

MILK LIKE SUGAR was first presented by La Jolla Playhouse, opening on August 30, 2011, at the Potiker Theatre in La Jolla, California, co-commissioned with Theater Masters and produced in association with Playwrights Horizons and Women's Project Productions; with sets by Mimi Lien, costumes by Toni-Leslie James, lighting by Justen Townsend, sound and original music by Andre Pluess, production stage management by Dana Depaul, production management by Linda S. Cooper, and general management by Debby Buchholz. The director was Rebecca Taichman. The cast was as follows:

ANNIE	Angela Lewis
TALISHA	Cherise Boothe
MARGIE	Nikiya Mathis
ANTWOINE	LeRoy McClain
MALIK	J. Mallory McCree
MYRNA	Tonya Pinkins
KEERA	Adrienne C. Moore

MILK LIKE SUGAR was first presented in New York City by Playwrights Horizons, Women's Project, and La Jolla Playhouse, opening November 1, 2011, at The Peter Jay Sharp Theater; with sets by Mimi Lien, costumes by Toni-Leslie James; lighting by Justin Townsend, sound and original music by Andre Pluess, production management by Christopher Boll, and production stage management by Kyle Gates. The director was Rebecca Taichman. The cast was as follows:

ANNIE	Angela Lewis
TALISHA	Cherise Boothe
MARGIE	Nikiya Mathis
ANTWOINE	LeRoy McClain
MALIK	J. Mallory McCree
MYRNA	Tonya Pinkins
KEERA	Adrienne C. Moore

CHARACTERS

ANNIE

TALISHA

MARGIE

ANTWOINE

MALIK

MYRNA

KEERA

(A tattoo parlor. ANNIE, TALISHA *[nails like talons, lac-quered, bejeweled and bedazzled] and* MARGIE *[bubbly, dressed all in one bright color].)*

(Each girl receives many texts throughout, and each has her own specific text tone.)

TALISHA. It's gonna be mad cool, yo.

ANNIE. You think?

MARGIE. *(showing her tattoo)* It'll be just like mine.

ANNIE. *(leaning in to* MARGIE*)* Is that straight?

TALISHA. Of course it's straight.

MARGIE. I got mine from someone got his own tattoo place, *but* this dude here practices on oranges so it *is*, it's mad c –

ANNIE. Oranges isn't skin. I should wait.

TALISHA. You don't need to wait you need to lie down and choose your colors.

(A ring tone sounds.)

Yo that's a wacked out ring shit.

ANNIE. *(looking at caller ID)* Yo, that's called *culture*. Not every song invented got to be clubs and thugs and shit.

TALISHA. Well, if that's your moms tell her we out all night cause the party's right.

*(*ANNIE *hangs up the phone.)*

ANNIE. It's not my moms.

MARGIE. If that was *my* moms I better stay out all night cause next time she see me she hit me upside the back my head quick right.

ANNIE. This tattoo guy gets to use all the colors or just a couple?

TALISHA. 'Course he gets to use'm all. What you think this is, right? It's a tattoo shop, right?

ANNIE. It's not *his* tattoo shop, it's his cousin's –

MARGIE. He gets to use whatever he wants.

ANNIE. Well then what's up with this cat yo? What 's he gonna take all night?

TALISHA. So if it wasn't your moms; maybe it Malik.

MARGIE. Ooooo, Malik. I seen how he be lookin' at you Annie –

ANNIE. Give me water.

(**MARGIE** *takes a bottle of Alize out and hands it to* **ANNIE,** *who takes a seasoned swig.*)

TALISHA. What you getting, anyway?

(*A text for* **TALISHA.**)

MARGIE. Malik's mad cool.

ANNIE. Ladybug.

MARGIE. *(squeals)* Cute.

ANNIE. Malik's alright I guess.

TALISHA. A ladybug's kinda stupid.

ANNIE. I like ladybugs.

MARGIE. You guess? Why I go through all this trouble settin you two up for your birthday if you not diggin' on Malik?

ANNIE. When I say that? *(indicating bottle)* Water.

TALISHA. *(derisive)* Ladybug: It's like a little girl.

ANNIE. You kinda pissin' me off, Talisha.

TALISHA. It's T now. I'm so cool I don't even need a regular name like you all got, all I need is a 'nitial. T.

(**TALISHA** *holds up her arms as if she is flexing both arms, in the shape of a T.*)

ANNIE. You don't want us to use your real name?

TALISHA. Just call me T, now, okay?

MARGIE. Malik got one of them Slider phones real, real nice. Almost as nice as one of those Blackberry ones.

ANNIE. This kid better come give me my tattoo a-sap or I'm about to jet, yo.

MARGIE. You seen that slider phone?

TALISHA. Slider phones is kaput. Anyone can get them. And ladybug *is* like a little girl. There's a song about them. Remember that song kids sing about the ladybugs?

MARGIE. Tuh: I like that Slider phone.

ANNIE. If this tattoo kid so good how come he letting me get this shit for free? If he's so good he should wanna get paid, right?

TALISHA. Ladybug, ladybug, rings and rosie. Ladybug, ladybug, rings around the poses.

MARGIE. You high alright. No more for you.

TALISHA. That's it, that's it, right? That nurseries rhyme.

ANNIE. There ain't no such thing as a nurse*ries* rhyme.

TALISHA. Um, newsflash, school let out hours ago. This ain't English class.

ANNIE. *(playful)* Well shut up about nurseries rhymes and give me water, yo.

TALISHA. Which reminds me I gotta find out who gonna write my papers this year.

ANNIE. Yeah, last term your report card look like the side of a milk carton. D, D, D, D…

(The girls laugh.)

TALISHA. Yeah, that fool didn't even type the damn shit.

ANNIE. Where is this kid?

TALISHA. Sing that song with me.

MARGIE. Ms. Jones down the hall watched me I didn't go to no nurseries school.

TALISHA. Come on. Ladybug, ladybug…

*(*TALISHA *waits, then finally:)*

ANNIE. Your house is on fire your children will burn.

TALISHA. Your children will burn? What kind of shit is that for kids to sing?

ANNIE. Kids aren't supposed to sing it.

TALISHA. Well adults sure as hell don't go around singing it. What adult goes around singing shit?

ANNIE. I think it was made up like in old times like when women was first going to work and stuff. To make them feel bad just for leaving the house and crap.

TALISHA. What you mean women couldn't leave the house and crap, course women could leave the house, what person just stay inside the house like they in the zoo?

ANNIE. Like to work: they made that shit up to scare people.

MARGIE. When my mom went to work, Ms. Jones kept us *all* day.

(*A text for* MARGIE.)

Breakfast, lunch, sometimes dinner –

TALISHA. What a song about a insect got to do with scarin' people?

MARGIE. That spider song with the curdles and whey sure used to scare the hell out of me.

TALISHA. I only asked to know the words, shit.

MARGIE. Even though a flip phone's all Jerome got we still do it cause one day he gonna have a better one, right. One day maybe he have a touch screen. That what I think about: the future: when he got a touch screen. Those the kinds of things pop into your head when you pass one of them tests, you all: the future.

ANNIE. How many times you had to do it to pass?

MARGIE. Me and Jerome we do it all the time.

ANNIE. No, how many times you got to do those tests?

TALISHA. Supposed to be the morning pee, that's the best kind to make it come out right.

MARGIE. I think me and Jerome must be real what you call like fertile right? We like the way they is in the wild –

ANNIE. The wild Margie?

MARGIE. 'Cause I only got to take that test one time and BAM that Coach diaper bag almost mine, y'all.

TALISHA. How you afford a Coach anything, Margie?

MARGIE. You put what you want on a list. Then everyone you invite to your party has to buy things off that list. That's how it's done, I didn't make that up. Coach diaper bag –

TALISHA. Uh-uh, Burberry better.

MARGIE. A *Coach* diaper bag what I need for this baby to look good enough to be seen in public with me. Jerome already buy it little pink Jordans for its feet.

ANNIE. Burberry make sneakers, too. Match the scarf and the bag and the hat.

MARGIE. *And* I also want one of those jogger strollers.

TALISHA. Oooooo yeah. Those slick.

MARGIE. They slick cause they got the three wheels. So fancy four wheels be too much for those things.

TALISHA. Me too right. That's what I'd want too, right. In pink right.

ANNIE. Pink yeah. The army kind.

TALISHA. What? Camouflage.

ANNIE. Yeah, yeah. Me, too, yeah.

MARGIE. Yeah.

TALISHA. Mad cool.

ANNIE. *(to* **TALISHA***)* Maybe you and me should hit ourselves up with some baby juice like Margie here.

MARGIE. Coach bags for all of us.

TALISHA. My mom kill me if I come home with a baby. Like she bring out that extension cord for real.

ANNIE. Yo. Won't need moms no more if we each have tiny little babies made just for us, right?

MARGIE. Yeah, y'all, you two do this too and we have one big old *huge* shower for all three of us y'all.

TALISHA. How we all have a baby at the same time, yo? That kind of shit got to be planned out. What we need would be like charts and thermometers and shit.

MARGIE. Hey, I got PG and I didn't have no kind of fever any the times me and Jerome hit it.

TALISHA. We'd need thermometers, I seen it.

ANNIE. We don't need no thermometers and we don't need no charts, we just need it to be the right time and for me I know it the perfect time. I read once where it only work like once a month. Like clockwork I get mine whenever my dad change the oil on his cab and he due at Jiffy Lube next week. I remember cause that how I get out of going since he make me keep him company. I say cramps and he damn near lock the doors on me, so it work like a charm and I don't have to go *no*where.

MARGIE. I bet a camouflage stroller be the kind Beyonce have 'cause she all strong like.

ANNIE. We all have babies we could be like, like strong and fierce just like that. Just like lions. Hunting around at night.

TALISHA. Surrounded by cute little cubby babies all day.

MARGIE. Yeah, yeah.

TALISHA. So, if we all gonna do this, you should get a rose since me and Margie both already got a rose.

MARGIE. This be real cool, yo, if Annie meet up with Malik, and you hurry it up with whoever's your flavor of the moment old dude –

TALISHA. He ain't old he just ain't no kid.

MARGIE. A red rose'll match our nails *and* Malik's phone.

ANNIE. Maybe I don't want everything all the same color and shit.

MARGIE. You sayin' I don't look good? I look *good* yo. This is style yo.

ANNIE. I do like red.

TALISHA. We all get red roses and we all do this baby thing. Okay?

ANNIE. And a ladybug is red.

TALISHA. A ladybug is stupid.

MARGIE. You both gotta get your move on, right, if we want to have our girls all at the same time.

TALISHA. Yo, Sierra and Cassie both got PG before school let out last year they already seen theirs on a screen but they did it all wrong. I seen them at McDonald's before school and you not supposed to eat breakfast if you want a girl. They did it all wrong and now they both stuck with boys. See Annie, you ain't the only one who can talk about shit.

ANNIE. You know, we don't even know if your dude got a name.

MARGIE. Who is it? Ramon? He got one of them sidekick things real slick.

TALISHA. I gets mine, that's all I'm at liberty to say. But what I *can* say is this new guy I'm talkin' to is so fine, it amazing we don't don't do it *all* the time. Cause he set up good, he got his own place –

ANNIE. Own place? Where his parents?

TALISHA. I don't care where they are. He ain't no silly kid, that's all you gotta know.

MARGIE. You better get working on Malik, Annie. You don't have time to waste on this, for real. I'm almost eight weeks already so we gotta plan that party, y'all.

(**ANTWOINE** *enters, on the phone, which is of the flip variety. He shuts it, tucks it in his pocket.*)

ANTWOINE. Sweet sixteen right?

(*The girls get a bit shy.*)

(*With a jut of his chin,* **ANTWOINE** *indicates* **ANNIE** *lift her shirt.*)

(**ANNIE** *does, lies back, and* **ANTWOINE** *sits.*)

So what it gonna be?

TALISHA. She think she want a ladybug but I think that stupid, don't you think that kind of stupid?

ANTWOINE. I think she should get what she want to get.

TALISHA. Fine, then, ladybug, then; like a little girl.

MARGIE. Long as it's red. 'Cause then it match Malik's phone.

ANNIE. Like. Maybe like a little flame or something?

MARGIE. Ooo, that a good kind of red.

TALISHA. At least it's not some little girl crap.

ANNIE. Like you know when you light a match? Like when I see my dad light one of his smokes. That first flash a red right after the blue.

(ANTWOINE looks at ANNIE.)

ANTWOINE. Red after the blue. I like that.

TALISHA. But she don't want it blue. She want it red.

ANTWOINE. This gonna be forever yo, better be what you want, right?

(ANNIE looks at ANTWOINE.)

(ANTWOINE looks at ANNIE.)

(an understanding mixed with something else)

TALISHA. We don't got all night for this so maybe fill that thing up with the red and start right?

(ANNIE looks at TALISHA.)

(The phone rings. MARGIE grabs it.)

ANNIE. Bet that my moms, bet she callin' to say Happy Birth –

MARGIE. *(as she checks caller ID)* Ain't your moms, it Malik. Giirrrrrrllll, you better talk to this boy, shit.

(MARGIE hands the phone to ANNIE.)

ANNIE. *Yello.......*Fine. Just don't be late, yo.

(She hangs up.)

You gotta show them who's the boss, you know. I'm gonna get this thing d double done, yo.

(to ANTWOINE and with flourish:)

Flame. Red. I got places I need to be.

ANTWOINE. *(as he leans in and* **ANNIE** *lowers a corner of her jeans)* Alright then.

(The girls quiet as **ANTWOINE** *leans in to work.)*

ANTWOINE. *(almost to himself, filler conversation)* Fire's cool. Flame. Heat. Least it ain't no rose, right? A girl comes in here asks for a rose I know she ain't put much thought into this at all right, cause a rose ain't that special right?

MARGIE. A rose is real pretty.

TALISHA. Yeah, um, Annie got somewhere to be soon so you should probably hurry up.

ANTWOINE. A tattoo is work, right? It takes time, right?

*(**ANTWOINE** works.)*

ANNIE. So…um…you do this a lot?

ANTWOINE. Sure.

ANNIE. Like on real people a lot?

ANTWOINE. *(a twinge of a smile)* …yeah, I work on real people. I like a living canvas right. You take something like a person's arm, leg, and make it look like it ain't supposed to look but it's still beautiful, right?

ANNIE. Cool.

TALISHA. Yeah, neat-o, can we stop this chit chat? Tattoos isn't supposed to be like the Oprah show, we don't got to let all ourselves bust out and get all warm and cozy with each other. Red. Flame. Take the needle out and do the damn thing.

ANNIE. She eat her Wheaties every morning that why she so aggressive like.

*(**ANTWOINE** goes back to his work.)*

MARGIE. You know what? I think we should all get matching baby bottles, too right. Along with the strollers. I think the WIC'll give em for free.

TALISHA. Miss T, here is in like Flynn.

ANNIE. For real, ya'll: Prada, Louis V –

TALISHA. Three pink joggers and our baby girls will go to nurseries school together.

ANNIE. This gonna be mad cool, yo.

TALISHA. How long could my mom's stay mad, right? After a week she'd let me back home, right?

ANNIE. We gonna be like *lions, y'all.*

ANTWOINE. *(leaning in to his work)* You gotta hold still, now.

TALISHA. *(wagging her head)* Your children will burn. That's some kind of wacked out shit, Annie.

ANNIE. Well we all ain't gonna sing that kind of stuff to ours, right? Little baby gonna love us all for us and we gonna do everything the right way for them. We call them *all* day on their birthday, right?

TALISHA. You meet up with Malik, by Friday it probably be done, right? By Friday.

ANNIE. For real, of course. Pinky swear.

> *(ANNIE holds up her pinky.)*

> *(ANNIE, TALISHA, and MARGIE pinky swear.)*

This the only present I need.

> *(The sound of the tattoo needle whirs.)*

ANTWOINE. Here we go.

> *(The sound of a park in the dead of night.)*

> *(A clearing. MALIK.)*

> *(ANNIE enters.)*

> *(Much of ANNIE's bravado is gone.)*

MALIK. You made it.

ANNIE. Took forever to walk up here.

MALIK. It's worth it, you'll see. Whole world seems a thousands times more beautiful when you see it from here.

> *(MALIK looks up into the sky, proud, then to ANNIE.)*

ANNIE. So like what? This supposed to be romantical or something?

MALIK. If you want.

ANNIE. Like stars and moonlight and shit?

MALIK. Sure.

ANNIE. Well didn't you think this out? You the one keep calling me.

MALIK. Margie say you like me. She gave me your number, told me to call – It can be romantical if you want it.

ANNIE. You got something to drink?

(**MALIK** *shakes his head no.*)

How we supposed to do this if you don't got something to drink?

MALIK. I had pay to help my moms.

ANNIE. Why? She sick or something?

MALIK. I just had to help her.

ANNIE. How you have a slider phone if you got a sick moms can't pay shit for herself and shit?

MALIK. I don't want to talk about my moms. That's not really romantical to talk about your moms you know. Talking about your moms ain't gonna get someone in the mood.

ANNIE. Well fine if there's nothing to drink I guess that's okay.

MALIK. That how you usually? Like with something to drink?

ANNIE. Nosy.

MALIK. I should have brought something.

ANNIE. Yeah, you should have.

MALIK. Next time.

ANNIE. You wish, dude.

MALIK. Margie say you like me.

ANNIE. You done this before Malik?

MALIK. Sure.

ANNIE. How many times?

MALIK. I was thinking it would be nice to look up at the sky together.

ANNIE. With Cassie last year and who else?

MALIK. Cassie? My boy say she don't wash and shit. I hit
     it with Cassie my shit stink, too. I really. Thought you
     like the sky.

ANNIE. Sky's the sky.

MALIK. Big dipper, little dipper and all that shit. Milky way.

ANNIE. You bring a blanket I don't want to get dirty.

MALIK. I –

ANNIE. Well shit, Malik.

MALIK. I don't think Margie knows what she say.

ANNIE. Nope. She don't.

   (*awkward*)

   Well may as well get started –

   (ANNIE *starts to unzip her pants.*)

MALIK. Oh. Right. Yeah.

ANNIE. Sky's the sky, Malik. Nothing special.

   (ANNIE *unbuttons her shirt halfway.*)

   Well come on.

MALIK. Sure.

   (MALIK *undoes his pants, stops.*)

ANNIE. Like what now?

MALIK. I thought you like the sky.

ANNIE. I never said I didn't like the sky.

MALIK. I kinda like searched for this place.

   (ANNIE *looks at* MALIK.)

ANNIE. You did?

MALIK. Margie told me you. Nevermind. This probably not
     what you like at all. You probably never even look at
     the sky. I should head back down –

ANNIE. Don't, don't do that –

MALIK. I real popular since I got this slider phone. You and
     Margie prolly see that and think.

ANNIE. You don't have to go, Malik.

MALIK. My moms sick.

ANNIE. C'mon, man, it's like my birthday, yo.

    (MALIK *stops.*)

    You got to be nice to me on my birthday, yo.

    (MALIK *waits.*)

    And. I. Notice the sky.

MALIK. ...Yeah?

ANNIE. ...Sure.

MALIK. I searched this place out, right.

ANNIE. It's real nice.

MALIK. Yeah?

ANNIE. Sure.

MALIK. *(excited)* Cause you can see like the constellations and shit from here. Lights from the city so far away you can really. From my window I can barely see anything real good, like real stars. I look up, think I see, then wham, it moves.

ANNIE. Maybe it's like a shooting one or something.

MALIK. Naw. It's usually just a plane. I squint enough I almost can see those people's faces, flying away, looking down at me. I squint more I can almost see one or two laughing. Like at me. In my window, wishing I was up there, too... shit.

ANNIE. What?

MALIK. I need to go. This ain't right.

ANNIE. I...like you Malik.

MALIK. You just want Margie and Talisha think we did something.

ANNIE. No. I. I like you.

    (ANNIE *looks at* MALIK.)

    (MALIK *looks at* ANNIE.)

MALIK. Yeah?

ANNIE. Sure.

    (ANNIE *smiles.*)

(MALIK *gets shy.*)

(ANNIE *walks up to* MALIK.)

(MALIK *inches a little closer to* ANNIE.)

(ANNIE *kisses* MALIK.)

(MALIK *kisses back.*)

MALIK. This don't have to do with my phone, do it?

(ANNIE *kisses* MALIK *harder.*)

(ANNIE *kisses* MALIK *almost too hard.*)

Hey.

ANNIE. I said I like you. Don't you like me too?

(ANNIE *kisses* MALIK *hard, reaches for his zipper.*)

MALIK. HEY.

ANNIE. Like what the fuck, yo?

(MALIK *looks at* ANNIE.)

MALIK. You tryin'a hit it pretty quick, yo.

ANNIE. How many times I got to say I *like* you, *dag?*

MALIK. You diggin' at me like I'm some sort of grab bag at a kiddie party, right.

ANNIE. You beginning to waste my time, Malik.

MALIK. You don't even ask me do I got protection or nothin'. I ain't thinking about being somebody's daddy.

ANNIE. You don't need to worry about none of that with me.

MALIK. That's what you say *now.*

ANNIE. 'sides, if something happen, it could be just for me. Like only for me. You wouldn't have to do anything, not even change its diapers right?

MALIK. Nah, nah. I don't like those people up in that plane laughing at me. Cause the way I imagine it, they see me from my window, Annie. They see into my window, they see the paint curling off the walls, they see my mom ain't done the washing in weeks, they see there ain't more than two packages macaroni and cheese in the cupboard. They see that and they mouths crimp up into smiles and I wanna crush those smiles. 'Cause all they see is some bone head baby daddy don't know enough to use a rubber and end up stuck – paint curling, milk like sugar on the shelf. I do this like you want I be stuck forever with them laughing at me. Make my skin burn. You think about that? People like them folks in that plane up there? Laughing down at you like that? You and Talisha and all y'all can rot in this place but I won't. Thought you wouldn't want to, either.

(The sound of a plane overhead.)

(ANNIE and MALIK look up into the sky.)

(A breakfast table. [Kitchen scene is new/rearranged.])

(Morning light.)

(ANNIE eats a pop tart.)

(MYRNA writes in a notebook, is often lost in thought.)

ANNIE. You was happy when you had us, right?

MYRNA. Boom, boom, boom. One after the other. Like stair steps.

ANNIE. Cause I. See. Talisha and Margie and, we kinda made this. Promise. We gonna be like fierce lions –

MYRNA. What you still doing here? When school start?

ANNIE. Oh, I was thinking I get Daddy swing back and pick me up –

MYRNA. What wrong with the bus?

ANNIE. I know I'm not feeling that bus today –

MYRNA. City bus or you walkin' Anniegirl. What customers Daddy get if you sitting in there with him?

ANNIE. Bus just got lots of people on it.

MYRNA. That the *point* of the bus.

ANNIE. I don't know if I wanna be all up against all those... people, right?

(MYRNA writes.)

Nevermind.

(ANNIE *eats.*)

ANNIE. *(cont.)* Had a good birthday night.

MYRNA. That's good.

ANNIE. Didn't get…maybe I missed. I had the ringer on but maybe I missed your call, right?

MYRNA. Sunday we'll do something. Name it, we'll do it, Ms. Big Old Sixteen. Name it. What you want?

ANNIE. Thought. Maybe you'd call when you got a ten minute or something.

MYRNA. Smoke breaks go quick as a wink. You think you gonna get so much done and 'fore you light the dog gone thing, foom. It's all over. I told Daddy to call.

ANNIE. Daddy quit using the phone in the cab. Say he get better tips when he quit using the phone in the cab.

MYRNA. Well, there's only one of me, Annie.

ANNIE. …I know.

MYRNA. The boys up yet?

ANNIE. Already left.

MYRNA. Good for them to be out early. Hear they hiring down the public works, maybe the boys get lucky, get a job.

ANNIE. Maybe.

(ANNIE *eats.*)

(MYRNA *chuckles.*)

(ANNIE *stops eating, looks at* MYRNA.)

What's so funny?

MYRNA. Whole office quiet and it's just my fingers and those keys. Click, click, click.

ANNIE. So corner left his computer on again? That what happened to you?

MYRNA. Corner's a lady.

ANNIE. I don't think you should touch their stuff.

MYRNA. Picture of two kids in heavy frames on her desk and past few days I seen she got cookie wrappers in her rubbish bin. Thin mints cause those girl scouts been sellin' em down the bus station and she be going through them a box a day, so I think those two kids in those fancy frames gonna turn into three soon.

ANNIE. Just do the vacuum and get out there fast. Didn't they already like write you up about –

MYRNA. Their bark is worse than their bite. I think her office be empty soon cause who gonna keep her around she got a tiny baby at home? Babies is work –

ANNIE. Work? Not so much. You can dress 'em real nice. That's kinda what me and the girls – . Cause babies ain't like *real* work, they cuddly and cute and love you all for –

MYRNA. I don't know how cute it is to be changing diapers every two hours even in the middle of the night. The boys were the worst with that. Every two hours they'd just piss through everything, pamper, pajamas, sheets, everything. You wouldn't think baby pee would stink but it do if you leave it. I was so tired I'd leave it and my mother would come over and give me an earful as she sprayed the crib with the pine-sol. Naw, babies is a whole lot of work and then some. That lady with the girl scout cookies know all about it. And that office only have one other lady in there and her v-v probably got webs all up in it.

ANNIE. Ma.

MYRNA. Maybe, and this just a crazy thought, but maybe, when she go, they say, Myrna Desmond, we got this one office free, Myrna Desmond, maybe you see if you could make good use of it, since it free and all.

ANNIE. There no such thing as a "v-v."

MYRNA. How you know? Thought they take that sexy class out of the school when we all told them that our job to teach you all. *Our* job: not no school's job teach about the birds and the bees.

ANNIE. Last I checked birds and bees ain't got nothing to do with p-p's going into v-v's.

MYRNA. That mouth. I ought to have your father wash it with soap.

(*pause*)

I'm thinking if I can finish this one, I print it, I print all my stories out and make some copies – I have the key to that copy room, right? – and see if one them guys sell it down the bus station. I'm just as good as one of them girl scouts. I get maybe one your brothers draw something for the cover.

ANNIE. When the last time one of them drew anything?

MYRNA. They get that creative spirit from me.

ANNIE. They're too old to draw.

MYRNA. Never too old to have creative spirit. *You* got the pessimic that's what you got.

ANNIE. The pessimic?

MYRNA. I bet people like my stories.

ANNIE. I think it's called *pessimism.*

(**MYRNA** *blinks at this.*)

MYRNA. I bet I could even make movies out of my stories. I love the movies. Life all big in front of me. Blown up. Lose yourself.

ANNIE. No one else likes going to the movies anymore.

MYRNA. Who don't like the movies?

ANNIE. People next to you smell and stuff in there.

MYRNA. Who smells at the movies?

ANNIE. Bums and people.

MYRNA. What bum can pay to see a movie?

ANNIE. I'm just sayin. I went last night with the girls and I didn't lose myself, instead I really-

MYRNA. What was this? A late movie?

ANNIE. Yeah.

MYRNA. It got Denzel in it?

ANNIE. No, it ain't got Denzel in it, Ma –

MYRNA. That too bad, Denzel my *man.*

ANNIE. It didn't have Denzel and that's not what I'm tryina. What I. What I'm saying is, I was in that movie and I was. Seeing those faces above me like in the dark. Everything shiny and glossy and I'm looking up at the screen at those perfect faces – cause this kid, the one I was hanging with, he said this thing about. And I was thinking about… Maybe theres another way to. Be. Like you ever get confused about who you supposed to…? Like with the girls I'm like…but this kid was saying we shouldn't. But me and the girls came up with this plan, this like perfect plan…but I still feel there's maybe… Like another like, like the way people float by in like an airplane.

MYRNA. When you been on an airplane Annemarie Desmond?

ANNIE. I only said "like" an airplane.

MYRNA. Your Aunt Rae the only one been on one and she say it wasn't no great shakes.

ANNIE. Forget it.

MYRNA. Your Aunt Rae could turn heads. Met a guy said he get her on Star/Search –

ANNIE. Search. Yeah, I know.

MYRNA. Our ma used to say all a little girl need is be pretty and the world can crack open for her like a egg.

ANNIE. I don't want things cracking around me.

MYRNA. It an expression, Annie. And it true. Rae been on trips. Always got her nails polished and her hair done up. Aunt Rae buyin' Maybeline, I'm buying pampers: boom, boom –

ANNIE. I think I might like an airplane. Wouldn't you like to try –

MYRNA. You know I never wrote that one down?

ANNIE. You ain't even listening.

MYRNA. I been telling you about that egg I don't know how long and I think I shoulda written it down by now, don't you think?

(ANNIE *looks at* MYRNA.)

ANNIE. Guess I should get goin'.

MYRNA. Yeah. With the boys out, you gone –

ANNIE. The house is quiet for you, I know, but I'm. Just wondering if you was happy when you had us –

MYRNA. That school gonna call here if you don't hop to it. That new teacher with the fancy degree –

ANNIE. Yeah, she stapling college brochures to all our papers –

MYRNA. She one Nosy B, I tell you what. Summer barely gone she already all up in our business talking about tardy this, truant that. You was only out two days. What, you miss building space rockets in those lousy two days? "Brochures." Where she gonna be when that college bill come due? College expensive. You get a good job, pay your own bills, stay on the straight and narrow. What more you need? I always did love September though. All them books you get to take home, read up.

ANNIE. They just bo – . (an attempt at a joke) You can cuddle up to us more than some lousy books.

MYRNA. Airplanes, Maybelline: eggshell may as well been cement for me, ladybug.

ANNIE. Don't call me that, mom, it's like a little girl.

(The sound of a school yard.)

MYRNA. You always be my little girl. Sunday we'll do something.

ANNIE. Sunday, sure.

(A school bell ring.)

(The kitchen disappears.)

(A bank of lockers.)

(ANNIE, TALISHA, *and* MARGIE *work making their clothes as revealing and tight as possible as* TALISHA *does her nails and* MARGIE *does her hair.*)

(**KEERA** *in long modest skirt, modest blouse, stands slightly removed, back pack on her shoulders.*)

(**ANNIE** *looks down at her tattoo.*)

TALISHA. *(to* **KEERA***)* If you agree, then you can walk right?

ANNIE. *(to* **TALISHA***)* Cut that out, right?

TALISHA. Why you care right? *(to* **KEERA***) And* it need to be typed. Last kid I got to do this shit got me some bad grades yo. My mom nearly wore out her arm on me when that report card came in the mail.

ANNIE. Can't you just let her walk?

MARGIE. Who cares about English? What we should worry about is gym. We gonna be in delicate conditions yo.

TALISHA. *(to* **KEERA***)* One in history due Tuesday.

ANNIE. Just finish your nails and let's go, right?

TALISHA. Tuesday.

KEERA. Tuesday, okay.

TALISHA. Why you care about Miss Holly Hobbie here?

(a text for **MARGIE***)*

ANNIE. We just gonna be late right?

MARGIE. I don't think I should be messing around with mother nature, right? By exercising and shit?

TALISHA. No, no exercise supposed to be real good. Only thing you can't do is ride horses and shit. I seen that in the movies. You do shit like that you bleed and you lose it. Then we got to start over.

(to **KEERA***)*

Hey, you even know what this paper supposed to be about yo? If I were you I'd get a pencil out and take some notes and shit. It gotta be good.

(**KEERA** *rummages in her bag for a pencil and paper.*)

MARGIE. If you two is in this you all better hurry yourselfs up.

TALISHA. You get it done with Malik?

ANNIE. Malik making this all harder than it need to be, so I been thinking 'bout talkin up someone else.

TALISHA. Someone like who?

ANNIE. We shouldn't be talking about all this stuff out here.

(**KEERA** *looks up.*)

KEERA. Oh, it's okay, I wouldn't say nothin'.

TALISHA. What you spring cleaning in there? Shit. Pencil, paper, so you can get gone and stop taking up our air.

ANNIE. Talisha –

KEERA. I'm just. Can't find.

(*A small radio falls out of* **KEERA**'s *bag.*)

(**TALISHA** *grabs for it.*)

TALISHA. This like from olden times shit.

KEERA. It just til I get a new one. My dad gonna get me a new one for Christmas coming up –

ANNIE. (*to* **TALISHA**) Give it back. First bell gonna ring any minute.

(**TALISHA** *plays with it, teases.*)

TALISHA. (*makes static sound as she pretends to tune the radio*) You get this Annie?

(**TALISHA** *plays with radio, then finally gives it back.*)

Why you carry around a big huge bag for no reason if you ain't got good stuff in it for real?

KEERA. Maybe I got a pencil in the bottom. I'm slow as molasses, my mother do say.

TALISHA. Well she right.

(*waves at* **KEERA**)

You can walk on, long's you do that paper.

(*to* **ANNIE**)

We can make Malik come around. How bout I have my guy rough him up a bit?

MARGIE. How she hit it with Malik if he all bruised and shit?

ANNIE. Maybe you all keep your voices down, right?

KEERA. I wouldn't say nothing, promise. Not if it supposed to be y all's secret right. My cousin got two babies already and they real sweet when they not sick.

MARGIE. Wait. How much her tests cost? Cause mines *cost.*

KEERA. Mad money. If you all have babies I hope they way cuter than my cousin's babies cause they took after the fathers so if you all havin some of you own better make sure the daddy cute cause it's like the inside of a twinkie: sometimes just like you expect, other times not enough frosting. Nothing worse than a twinkie without frosting and nothing sadder than a ugly baby.

(All three girls look at **KEERA.***)*

Just. Hope your babies ain't ever sick an come out not ugly 's what I mean.

TALISHA. Like a twinkie.

KEERA. Yeah –

*(***TALISHA*** looks at* **KEERA,** *who does not move.)*

MARGIE. Like seriously, I don't want my baby deformed or no such thing cause I climbed some stupid ass rope in gym class, yo.

KEERA. Exercise could be a real good thing, actually. A lady in one of the churches I went to before I moved here used to walk all up and down Massachusetts Avenue and her baby could run before his first birthday.

TALISHA. I am like still wondering who told you you were in this conversation?

MARGIE. What Massachusetts Avenue got to do with babies who walk too much? And mine ain't gonna do that, I'm gonna train her to be good and sit in that stroller. This street walking baby sound like a bad baby. I don't want my baby come out running all around like a running fool. 'Cause I'm pretty sure it matters what you do when they in there. My mama went water skiing when she was pregnant with my older brother and his head way flat, yo. Flat, *flat,* flat.

ANNIE. That's ridiculous, Margie.

TALISHA. It is too. I seen it, Annie.

KEERA. I could see how that could happen right, yeah? I could see –

(**TALISHA** *lifts her hand up in a stop gesture to* **KEERA**.)

TALISHA. *Why* does your mouth keep *moving*?

KEERA. But I know lots about babies since they lettin' me teach Sunday school at my new church –

TALISHA. *(turns back to* **KEERA**) Tuesday you have my paper or walking around up in here gonna get real rough for you.

MARGIE. I carryin' the future around in here. I should get notes for the whole rest of the year.

KEERA. I wouldn't tell no one.

TALISHA. Not me. I gonna sign up for extra gym. Exercise real good, right Annie?

KEERA. Really, I can keep a secr –

TALISHA. You better watch it, Holly Hobbie. You takin up too much air.

(*The school bell rings.*)

MARGIE. My brother cute but I can't have a baby like that uh uh, I'ma see about my notes.

(**TALISHA** *ushers* **MARGIE** *away. They exit.*)

(*As* **ANNIE** *starts to go:*)

ANNIE. Sorry about Talisha.

KEERA. At my last school one girl spiked my lunch milk with dollar perfume, so Talisha ain't *so* bad. Thanks for showing me the bathroom when school first started.

ANNIE. I should go –

KEERA. I won't tell no one about you all's plan if you really tryina keep it a secret, don't worry.

(*a text for* **ANNIE**)

ANNIE. See you, right?

KEERA. Eventhough, I kinda think the family supposed to be a special thing. My cousin treating it like it a patchwork quilt, piecing it together here and there with the different mens. How you honor your mother and father if that all they can do, is piece things together like that?

ANNIE. Maybe it the mother and the father should be honoring those babies.

KEERA. Two way street, you right.

ANNIE. Second bell gonna –

KEERA. Right, right. Don't want to be late, even if it only gym.

ANNIE. Yeah. I seen you in gym. You try to wear that skirt again you gonna get detention for real, yo.

KEERA. Always more than one way, my daddy say.

ANNIE. People make less fun of you if you didn't talk like one of those cat posters in the library.

KEERA. Sometimes there're two or three excellent ways, my daddy say all the time. I was just taught different, that's all. My whole family honor me enough to teach me different.

ANNIE. My family does all right.

KEERA. When was the last time you each sat at the table together and all ate? Together.

ANNIE. My brothers go out a lot.

KEERA. With those womens, right?

ANNIE. And my moms works nights.

KEERA. Sound like there ain't a lot of family purity going on in your house, if you ask me. My house? Dinner at six every night. On the dot. Whole meal with each kind of food you supposed to have laid out for us all to share. First thing I think when I hear about those strollers, first question I ask myself was, I asked myself, "Keera?" and myself say, "Yes?" And I say, "Keera, when the last time those girls eat good foods with they family like you do?" And my self say, "Probably been a long time, Keera, probably been a long, long time."

(a text for ANNIE*)*

KEERA. *(cont.)* Best thing to do about those strollers is sit deep inside yourself and pray on it.

ANNIE. They so loud about it.

KEERA. Your girl Margie so excited she been facebooking about it all night.

ANNIE. Dag that was fast. Haven't checked it in a minute. Hold up, how you get Margie friend you on Facebook?

KEERA. I friended Shanea and I keep up through her. Shanea want eight hundred friends by Christmas.

ANNIE. Yeah, she friend anybody.

KEERA. So I know all about everything. But my cousin got only five things off her list and not one of them was Coach, just so you know.

ANNIE. It could be mad cool.

KEERA. Everyone around us want Jordan's right? But I think. I think maybe our feet ain't *meant* to wear Jordans.

ANNIE. You right. Jordans suck. Adidas better.

KEERA. No, like what if our feet meant to wear slippers of white satin, right? Every spring? My daddy and me go to this special father-daughter dance where he pledge his fatherly devotion to me. It's the, the *bomb*, right? He wears his best suit and I wear a ball gown right? And white satin slippers. Cause maybe we never meant to wear no sneakers. No sneakers at all ever cause they kinda evil.

ANNIE. How a sneaker evil?

KEERA. How a sneaker fill your soul? Maybe our hearts is so pure Jordan's burn our feet, right? You got to think of yourself like that Annie. A pure heart. To be protected. You should pray on it.

ANNIE. I'm not real religious like.

KEERA. Me neither, really. Half the time I pray my mom makes cheesecake for dessert or something you know silly like that. Don't need to be religious, just gotta change your way of thinking. It'll. It'll feel so good it'll almost make you soar. Like above everyone like free like a. Dove or something.

ANNIE. Soar above, I, I like that. And that sneaker thing. Pure heart and all. Got this tattoo for my birthday and ever since that needle I sure been. Thinking –

(The school bell rings.)

KEERA. I have a more excellent way.

*(**ANNIE** touches her side where her tattoo is.)*

The clearing.

*(**MALIK**.)*

*(**MALIK** looks up at the sky.)*

(The sound of an airplane overhead.)

(Lights up on the tattoo parlor.)

*(**ANNIE**, **TALISHA**, and **MARGIE** sharing another bottle of bright liquor as before.)*

*(**ANTWOINE** looks over **ANNIE**'s new tattoo.)*

*(**MARGIE** and **TALISHA** text.)*

ANTWOINE. Uh-uh, Sweet Sixteen. No way. That ain't healed from last time, right. I do it over and it gonna hurt like hell, yo.

ANNIE. I got birthday money from my aunt. I can pay this time.

ANTWOINE. It's gonna take up half your stomach.

ANNIE. I just need it bigger.

ANTWOINE. You serious.

TALISHA. *(texting)* Yeah she serious or why we hang out here for no reason?

ANNIE. Please?

ANTWOINE. I been doing this so long in my head barely used to someone wanting me to really get goin' on them like this. I did it once though. Created something from nothing. Had a cat in this chair asked me to do a boat. Well, bigger than a boat, a ship. You know, sails and poles holding them up and waves of water and even mermaids and shit. I don't think this cat'd even been on the Amtrack, maybe only ever heard salt's in the ocean. Never felt it himself. Never smelled it himself. But now he get to go there everytime he look down, right? Something from nothing and that cat thinks he part of the world now, all cause of me. I rippled that cat's skin into waves, right? I can move people, change people –

TALISHA. *Tuh.*

ANTWOINE. Aw. Shit. Listen to me go. Lemme see what kind of colors my cousin got for me to work with.

(*ANTWOINE exits.*)

(*ANNIE looks down at her tattoo.*)

(*MARGIE texts.*)

(*TALISHA texts.*)

TALISHA. It's Thursday night, 'case you didn't know.

(*a text for* MARGIE)

ANNIE. I know.

TALISHA. And? So? You talk sense to Malik?

MARGIE. (*texting*) Jerome wanna know we wanna meet up. He say you can even bring your old dude if you want.

TALISHA. For the last time he's not *old*, he just ain't a kid like you all gots.

MARGIE. He old or he wouldn't send those kinds a texts.

ANNIE. Is he like some pervert or something?

MARGIE. He a pervert if he into the foods. He send T texts about doing things in jell-o and craziness.

TALISHA. Yo, this is my dude to handle yo, not you alls.

ANNIE. He's totally a pervert or something.

TALISHA. What's nasty about jell-o little kids eat it all the time?

MARGIE. He a big old pervert if he into the foods.

TALISHA. What you know about the foods?

MARGIE. Foods ain't got nothing to do with anything. He confused about how everything supposed to work when you doing it if he start up talking about foods. I know about these things. I'm the one preggo, right? Shoot, didn't you take health with all the rest of us? When they talk about food?

(TALISHA *stops texting and considers.*)

ANNIE. They did bring in that banana.

(TALISHA *begins texting again.*)

MARGIE. Yeah, I don't know why they bring that into girls health we not the ones need to know how to use those things. That nurse don't know nothing about nothing, let me tell you. Brought in that banana and all those rubbers but how that gonna teach us about the real thing? Banana don't talk. Banana don't make excuses. Banana pretty much do what you want it to do.

ANNIE. Margie, it's a banana. It *always* gonna do what you want it to.

TALISHA. *(to MARGIE regarding the pervy texts)* You right. I just sent a reverse smile face.

MARGIE. Yo that's called a frown, dummy.

TALISHA. Who you Annie all the sudden? Think you smarter than everyone else?

ANNIE. What that supposed to mean?

MARGIE. You shouldn't talk to old dudes.

TALISHA. *(to ANNIE)* You just get high and mighty and shit is all.

ANNIE. Who high and mighty?

TALISHA. Who raise their hand in class today like some punk Poindexter? You see that Margie? I nearly fell out my seat laughing at her punk ass.

ANNIE. I…I guess it was stupid.

TALISHA. Yeah it was stupid. You just supposed to get it done with Malik, not start actin' like the damn kid.

MARGIE. Don't old dudes smell and stuff?

TALISHA. They not that old they *smell*, Jesus, Margie.

ANNIE. You know, *you* the one high or you wouldn't be texting every Mr. Magoo on the frickin world wide web to come take your clothes off.

MARGIE. Clothes off? That's kinda gross. You don't need them all off to do it. You crazy or something that's like what a ho would do, take all her clothes off and shit. Gross.

TALISHA. Well who you talking to ' you so nosy about me?

ANNIE. I'ma take my time I don't want my baby have half the genes of some bum from just anywhere.

TALISHA. Malik be talking to Shanea Twymon now.

ANNIE. What you mean "now", that was like a day ago.

TALISHA. You must of done something wrong or something.

ANNIE. You know his moms sick?

TALISHA. His moms ain't the one got to stick it in, Annie. Who the fuck cares?

ANNIE. Grow a heart, Talisha.

TALISHA. It's T and *you* should grow some *balls* and fucking *do* this already 'cause Margie already passed hers. And while you pussy footin' around, yours truly Miss T here just. Passed. Hers.

(**TALISHA** *pulls a pregnancy test stick, out of her bag, complete with packaging.*)

(**MARGIE** *starts screaming in joy.*)

BAM.

MARGIE. Oooooo. Oooooo.

TALISHA. How you like them apples, Anniegirl? You better get a move on now or you gonna be all alone for real when me and Margie here have our shower, right Margie?

MARGIE. Ooooooooooooooooo.

ANNIE. You passed?

TALISHA. Sure as shit I passed.

ANNIE. How you pass we just planned this all out yesterday?

TALISHA. I'm just special like that. Holly Hobbie said they was money so after school I went and swiped em so I'd be ready. But I got to thinking. How some piss tell you you PG? What kind of fucked up shit is that? That's like space shit and stuff. So I tried it to see and Ba-AM. Like I said.

(TALISHA *and* MARGIE *laugh.*)

Malik your only chance since you done pissed off all the other boys we know with your smart ass self.

ANNIE. I'm just saying maybe the kid's got too much to worry about with his sick moms and all.

TALISHA. Or maybe you don't want a shower with us, maybe you don't like cake. Maybe you never eat cake.

ANNIE. I eat cake. Everybody eat cake.

TALISHA. How I know what you eat?

ANNIE. How long we tight?

MARGIE. *(does not look up from texting)* Since the seventh grade when we three the only one grew boobies over the summer.

ANNIE. So, way back. We been tight since way back, so I wouldn't break no promise –

TALISHA. "But."

ANNIE. Maybe Malik ain't the right one for this.

(*a text for* MARGIE)

TALISHA. Well who the fuck the right one? This tattoo guy? That be a joke. You see how he got that lame ass flip phone like that?

MARGIE. You deserve better than a lame ass flip phone, Annie.

TALISHA. *(to* ANNIE*)* You goin' back.

ANNIE. I'm not, I'm just thinking what if our Jordan's supposed to be slippers, like.

TALISHA. Are you on crack?

MARGIE. I told Jerome come meet us and he want to know why we here again. He say tattoo give him the creeps can we meet him at the Krispy Kreme instead.

TALISHA. What is so special about Jerome's shit that you have to smell it every two hours?

(ANTWOINE *enters with colors, takes a look at* ANNIE*'s tattoo, holds a red bit of color up to* ANNIE*'s body.*)

ANTWOINE. This ain't it.

(ANTWOINE *exits.*)

TALISHA. He all actin' like he Picasso.

ANNIE. Maybe he is like that, like an artist.

TALISHA. No he's not he does tattoos. Don't tell me you fell for all that living paper crap.

ANNIE. I. Think that's kinda. Cool, you, you know? As soon I took off the bandage when I got home I really looked down at that flame, and I thought this is good, right. I traced the edges of it with my finger and it was like I could feel under my finger nail get all warm, right? Like I really think maybe if he did it bigger –

(*a text for* MARGIE)

'Cause this cat like knows what he wants to. He has like a thing he's good at and he's doing it, right? How many people around here can say they special, can say they did that? That's –

TALISHA. So if you like this dude so much use him 'stead of Malik. Hell, use that homeless dude we always see at the movies.

MARGIE. You ain't backin' out Annie, right?

ANNIE. ...Maybe I just need to think on some stuff for a minute. Like maybe we meant to do something else, something different. Than this promise –

TALISHA. WHAT?

(long pause)

(a text for **MARGIE***)*

(pause)

(a text for **MARGIE**, *then finally:)*

MARGIE. *(yelling into her phone)* KRISPY KREME TWENTY DUMB ASS.

(to **ANNIE***)*

This minute better not last too long, Annie. Right T?

TALISHA. Better not.

MARGIE. Ooooo, pink y'all.

TALISHA. So we out? *(***TALISHA** *readies herself to go.)* If you go back on your word life's gonna get awful lonely for you, that's for damn sure. What kind of friend are you if you go breaking –

ANNIE. I am not breaking, I am thinking –

TALISHA. Yeah, well think on this: you about to fuck everything up for real. You wanna sit alone at lunch like Holly Hobbie? You want to stay home with your moms like Malik? Oh, that's right, I forgot, your moms don't care enough to even call you on your birthday, she don't even care you exist. You gonna do this Annie. It's called friendship. Look it up it's called loyalty. Or ain't we tight no more, Annie? Ain't we tight?

*(***ANNIE** *touches her tattoo.)*

(Music rises, rises, then gives way to the soft sound of an airplane in the night sky.)

(Quiet.)

(The clearing.)

(An older model telescope sits on a rickety tripod.)

*(***MALIK** *stands at the telescope, looks up into the night sky.)*

(A blanket is spread on the ground.)

(A basket sits near the blanket.)

(**ANNIE** *regards the blanket, the basket.*)

MALIK. This time I. Um. Came prepared.

(**ANNIE** *looks at the telescope.*)

You like it? I bought it off that little Chinese guy has the shop on the corner. Next to Frankie's? Frankie a cool cat, don't ask kids for ID or nothing I found out. I don't usually drink –

ANNIE. I figured as much Ranger Rick. Look, why you callin' me? I don't –

MALIK. And, and I, I got you some choices.

(*He moves to the basket, brings out three brightly colored bottles.*)

Blue, orange, or red. Frankie say the green make you sick you mix it with the others, so I didn't buy no green. Or. Or. If you not ready for a drink, we can look at the sky. Like a date?

ANNIE. Shanea like telescopes?

MALIK. What? I figure it almost like an extra curricular like colleges look for people to have. Stead of just basketball or football like they expect us to do.

ANNIE. Cause if Shanea like telescopes I don't know why we up here, Malik.

MALIK. Shanea flunked her last two Spanish tests even though her mom Puerto Rican: I ain't thinkin' about Shanea.

(**MALIK** *looks at* **ANNIE.**)

I saw you at your locker.

ANNIE. Like me and six hundred other people. Everyone got a locker, Malik.

MALIK. After your English class with your paper Dr. Fitzgerald hand back. It had one of those brochures she staples on the top page. Everyone else crumples theirs up but not you. Yesterday I saw you take a peek.

(*finally:*)

ANNIE. One college next to a river. You can learn how to row boats and shit. I never done that.

(**MALIK** *looks at* **ANNIE.**)

MALIK. Kinda impressed me that you took a peek.

(**ANNIE** *gets shy, looks at the telescope.*)

ANNIE. How you eat government cheese and you buying telescopes and shit?

MALIK. See, see: I knew you'd like it. Try it.

ANNIE. I...don't want to break it or nothin'.

MALIK. You won't. Just look through into it, this big huge sky gets shaped down to a little circle you can almost touch.

ANNIE. How you know so much about telescopes?

MALIK. ... Found a box under my mom's bed once. Stuff my dad left. One a big book of the constellations. Had his name written in it in pencil. A little smudged. Took that book out the box and kept it. My mom didn't even know the difference...

ANNIE. She okay your moms?

MALIK. ...She okay, sure.

ANNIE. *(attempt to change the topic)* ...For real, how you get this thing?

MALIK. She doesn't always use all her pills. So when she not using them no more I collect em and sell em and I bought that myself fair and square. Kinda. I'm glad I was wrong about you.

(**ANNIE** *smiles.*)

(**MALIK** *smiles.*)

(**MALIK** *kisses* **ANNIE.** *Sweet.*)

ANNIE. You shouldn't be eavesdropping on people like that.

MALIK. Not eavesdropping if you not saying anything. I'm thinking maybe I give you a hand cause I'm a senior, not a dinky sophomore like you.

ANNIE. College expensive.

MALIK. Those brochures be like plane tickets, Annie.

ANNIE. I read and shit, but my marks and stuff ain't so good for all that

MALIK. You got time. Next term, make better marks.

ANNIE. These teachers are chumps. We got the same books my mom had here.

MALIK. A book a book: you open the cover, you read whatever it is. It lead you to a next one and that one'll be better.

ANNIE. Books're tricky…tricky things. Used to keep mine in the kitchen. "I know this one," my mom says one time. Got all excited. Went through all the pages. Got all – . Probably could barely read it back in the day, and she sure as hell can't really now – . I stood there listening, her fingers tracin' over the type. Her voice searching. I don't leave no books out no more. Made me feel – . She looked up once she realize she could barely read it, her eyes nearly – . Her lookin' at me like that I felt like my whole chest just sitting there open, like she could see something in me don't smell right to her. Couldn't tell what – . …She stood there. Stood there. Then she shut that book quick. She pretty much always got house stuff for me to do after that. She think it time for homework, all sudden it time for the pine-sol. Shoot. That better than seeing her with that book. Try not to bring up nothing like that ever now. I hear her talk about that stuff and I can't even – .

MALIK. Poppin' out babies before you can vote ain't for you.

ANNIE. I'm, I'm tryin' to find a more excellent way.

MALIK. Yeah, what way that?

ANNIE. There's only one of me, Malik, I can't know everything.

MALIK. You and me in college, that's all you got to know, to think about –

ANNIE. What college gonna think we so special?

MALIK. Plenty, plenty of 'em –

ANNIE. What college gonna think this rickety thing make up for anything?

MALIK. …it's…an idea.

ANNIE. No school gonna think this the astronomy club, Malik. You shouldna wasted your money, shoulda just gone down the Krispy Kreme had you a couple two for one specials, make much more sense than this rickety –

(MALIK *goes to the telescope, begins to fold it up.*)

MALIK. You can be real nasty, you know that? I'm…I'm tryina help you. I ain't interested in throwing away my ticket and staying around here the rest of my life, wasting away like the rest of you all.

ANNIE. What that supposed to mean?

MALIK. The world a beautiful place. If it knocks you lose, it your job to hold on tighter.

ANNIE. And how I do that?

(MALIK *sets the telescope back.*)

MALIK. Try it.

(ANNIE *goes to the telescope, but does not touch it.*)

Try.

ANNIE. Nah.

MALIK. What, you scared

(MALIK *removes the telescope from its stand, holds it out to* ANNIE.)

ANNIE. I ain't scared.

(MALIK *pushes the telescope towards* ANNIE.)

MALIK. You scared, you scared, you –

(ANNIE *pushes the telescope away hard.*)

(*And the telescope falls, breaks.*)

ANNIE. I –

MALIK. You deserve to be with Talisha and them. You're like my mother, worse than my mother: I tell her, I yell at her, "Take everything those doctors say to or you're always gonna be like this, it's never gonna get any better." And what she do? Nothing. Not one.... Whatever. I use her extra and I find ways out.

ANNIE. You ain't better than me, Malik.

MALIK. You know what, I don't like you, I just feel sorry for you.

(The sounds of the airplane overhead.)

(MALIK looks up as he exits.)

ANNIE. *(calling after him)* No school gonna let you come near it, that's for sure. They take one look realize you no better than the rest of us. You a joke just like the rest of us, no better, not one little bit.

(ANNIE touches her side, where her tattoo is.)

(The sound of fire rises quickly, then fades.)

(The kitchen.)

It be easier if I was Margie. She don't care what people think so she ain't got *no* fear, right? She don't seem to need to think about – . This is nice, talking just quiet like this. Talisha and everybody ain't so into really listening. This is real nice.

KEERA. Your friends need the Good Word. They need to sit down and have a good long conversation with their hearts stead of the home shopping channel.

ANNIE. What your dad say about someone like Talisha who ain't getting' to wear no satin slippers or nothing? He have something churchy to say to her?

KEERA. Well first he'd pray for her. Then, maybe he say something like um. Well, when my Aunt Josie makes new, well, you know, "friends" and brings em by, he usually says about those guys something like about loose women and how those who lie with loose women become one with that loose woman. And, Pastor at my church'd say something like "If I...um...If I...deliver up...deliver up my body to be burned and, and have not love, I gain nothing."

ANNIE. Your aunt just sit there in church letting people talk about her getting burned up?

KEERA. She don't come with me. With us. Which is a sad sad thing, if you ask me. My church got beautiful things to say.

ANNIE. It don't have like blankets on the windows or some such shit, do it?

KEERA. Stained glass. Tall as a mountain into the sky. Whatever place I move to, I search for the biggest, warmest, boldest church I can find.

ANNIE. Sounds real nice.

KEERA. Best part, is the music. If the words can't set you free, the music surely can. Like a dove. Like this.

(KEERA pulls her radio out of her bag.)

ANNIE. That don't even look like it could work no more.

KEERA. I'm gonna make a believer out of you yet, Annie.

(a text for ANNIE)

Talisha and Margie ain't got nothing on you once you believe, trust me.

(KEERA tunes the radio to gospel music.)

This my channel here, this my OOOOOOO.

(The song should be anything that could really move these girls to be joyful and sing. It might be a good idea to check out the music of large gospel choirs that use movement, something KEERA can use to get ANNIE to dance and move with her.)

(KEERA starts to dance, respectably.)

Best part of the service is the music.

(KEERA dances.)

You can't say you don't believe after you one with the music, Annie. Like this.

(KEERA shows ANNIE the dance.)

(ANNIE does the dance, timidly at first, then gets into it.)

(The girls laugh and dance and laugh.)

You feel it, Annie? You feel the spirit?

ANNIE. *(laughing)* I feel like I'm five.

KEERA. Wait for it, wait for it now –

    (The girls laugh and dance and laugh.)

    (ANNIE lightens almost.)

    (The girls laugh and dance and laugh.)

    (Until MYRNA enters.)

MYRNA. What I tell you about noise during the dayt –

KEERA. Hi, Mrs. Desmond –

ANNIE. Mom, this is Keer –

MYRNA. Can't hardly sleep with all this –

ANNIE. Sorry –

KEERA. Sorry, Mrs. Desmond.

    (The music plays.)

MYRNA. And I know I can't hardly hear myself think –

    (KEERA turns off the radio.)

ANNIE. We was just –

MYRNA. You seen my notebook?

    (MYRNA begins rummaging for her notebook.)

ANNIE. *(to KEERA)* Maybe you should –

KEERA. Joyful noise can be pleasing if you hoping to find something you lost. I know when I lose something, if I can, I might like to hear a joyful –

MYRNA. A joyful noise to me be no noise at all.

KEERA. Sometimes a joyful noise need to be let out, though.

ANNIE. Maybe you should –

    (MYRNA stops ANNIE by putting a hand up.)

MYRNA. That so?

KEERA. Sure is. Sure is so –

MYRNA. I don't think I like that.

KEERA. Maybe you just ain't heard the right joyful noise. Maybe –

MYRNA. Goddamn it that notebook was just here, I swear it.

KEERA. The Lord's name in vain ain't– I should really probably maybe. Unless you all having dinner. I could stay if you want. Lead a prayer.

MYRNA. I don't think I like that neither.

KEERA. Just a little prayer before you eat to make joyful noise unto the –

MYRNA. Prayer. Tuh. The only joyful noise needed before we eat around here is thanks to me and Mr. Desmond for working our tails off to put the food on the table in the first place.

ANNIE. Ma –

MYRNA. Well who else put that food there?

KEERA. Well, Mrs. Desmond, the Lord Jesus –

MYRNA. I don't' got the stomach for this right now.

KEERA. I mean, because he did give you the job that pays you the money to put food –

MYRNA. The Offices of Hale and Dorr gave me my job.

ANNIE. Ma, she means –

MYRNA. The Offices of Hale and Dorr pay me and *I* am the one put food on this table.

ANNIE. I'll catch you tomorrow, Keera, right?

KEERA. When I lose something sometimes it be cause my mind be just creep creeping toward idle…best thing is to pray on something or think on something real hard. Then you get the strength move, really move forward. There's a purity in that, don't you think? A strength – ?

(**MYRNA** *looks at* **KEERA**, *then goes back to searching.*)

MYRNA. I like to see the holy ghost fry some chicken up, I surely would.

KEERA. That what you all having tonight? Chicken?

(**MYRNA** *ignores* **KEERA**.)

ANNIE. Catch you?

(**ANNIE** *looks at* **KEERA**.)

KEERA. Oh, oh yeah, oh sure, but I could stay –

(**KEERA** *gathers her things, goes.*)

(**ANNIE** *waves at her.*)

(**KEERA** *smiles, waves back.*)

MYRNA. Hope I didn't leave it on the bus, *never* find it if I left it on there –

ANNIE. That Keera from school. She real into church and stuff.

(**ANNIE** *seems altered. She smiles to herself.*)

MYRNA. What's gotten into you?

ANNIE. Don't know. Maybe the spirit. Her church sound nice.

MYRNA. That cause you ain't in it. Once you sit in it, it all changes, it all switches around.

ANNIE. Maybe we give it a chance.

MYRNA. A chance. Tuh. What kind of chance the church give me huh? Told my mother I was in trouble on a Tuesday, had the minister over to talk to me and your father by Wednesday, Saturday I'm wearing my Sunday white patent leathers and holding Daddy's hands at the alter with that same minister telling all of everybody what kind of girl he thought I was, but how I was gonna make it all up getting married. I stood up there watching them all nod they heads like I evil itself tamed in white patent leathers. That minister had all *kinds* of things to say about me but I tell you what: wasn't him around here when you all was underfoot, always asking, needing, pulling. Felt like my skin was barely my own – What kind of chance they give me, those church folks? The spirit. Tuh. Who is this girl Keera?

ANNIE. She's new.

MYRNA. What her parent's names?

ANNIE. She's *new.*

MYRNA. So her parents don't have no names?

ANNIE. How am I supposed to know their names?

MYRNA. Fresh.

ANNIE. Well you don't ask about any other parents' names: I like her.

MYRNA. I don't. Telling me she gonna say a prayer up in here in my kitchen where *I* buy the food. *I buy the food.*

ANNIE. She and her parents real tight. Got game night even: Yahtzee.

MYRNA. I'd like to see you try to make the boys stay in for a game night.

(**ANNIE** *smiles/laughs.*)

ANNIE. Might be fun.

(**MYRNA** *smiles/laughs.*)

MYRNA. Might be.

ANNIE. Wouldn't have to be Yahtzee. Could be some other type of game. Go fish, dominoes, checkers even –

MYRNA. Me and Rae used to love us some checkers. Play it for hours.

ANNIE. Keera got all sorts of good ideas. She alright.

MYRNA. Long as she leave all that holy stuff at the door.

ANNIE. You, me, the boys, Daddy even: we have game night/Checkers.

MYRNA. Checkers.

(**MYRNA** *smiles.*)

ANNIE. Dinner, too.

MYRNA. Boys could stand to stay one night in here with me.

ANNIE. Exactly, yeah.

MYRNA. Well okay.

(**ANNIE** *looks at* **MYRNA**.)

(**ANNIE** *hugs* **MYRNA**.)

(**MYRNA** *is caught off guard.*)

(**MYRNA** *does not respond at first.*)

(*Finally* **MYRNA** *hugs back, but pulls away first.*)

ANNIE. Maybe we invite Aunt Rae, too. Do it up real nice, it could be even better than a birthday. It'd be better than any present ever.

MYRNA. ...well okay.

(ANNIE *smiles.*)

(ANNIE *begins to straighten up the kitchen.*)

ANNIE. Okay then.

(ANNIE *stops.*)

(ANNIE *smiles.*)

(ANNIE *touches her side where her tattoo is.*)

(KEERA.)

(*Dances as with her radio.*)

(ANNIE *watches.*)

(*The tattoo parlor.*)

(ANNIE, TALISHA, *and* MARGIE.)

(TALISHA *texts on a blinged out phone. We can't see her entire face.*)

MARGIE. ...Why that fucking nurse work there if she don't like us kids? Went for my notes, she shoo me– I go today she make me do some hospital test in her stink ass office and of course it say I PG and then she pull on rubber gloves like I got some skanky disease – Starts bringing out stuff to read about the food I should be eating and the tests they gonna give me and GED and Headstart for the daycare and income this and doctors bills that and, and I'm getting dizzy right? All I see is those sick-people rubber gloves moving around the room, piling papers on my lap. Like she don't want her skin touch mine. Like I got some – And I breathin heavy all I see is those gloves when should be seeing pink, I should be seeing– But. I snap out of it and yell to that old bat: *My moms hosting my shower right? Take this stuff and shove it down your throat, right?* Cause my mom gonna do all the invitations in pink. Back in my family's home country this normal, shit.

ANNIE. Yeah... all this confusing stuff, right?

MARGIE. My whole family gonna help, they all said.

TALISHA. Tonight's the night, Annie: Friday, right?

ANNIE. ...You. You all know I ain't even ever been on a boat? I think I might like a boat. Or an Amtrack train. What good I be to a baby if all I know is what I can see and touch?

TALISHA. Told you you don't eat cake.

ANNIE. That ain't fair.

TALISHA. Breaking your word ain't fair.

(*a text for* ANNIE)

MARGIE. You ruining our shower, Annie. My mom so excited she started knitting the first pink sweater.

TALISHA. Could be a boy.

MARGIE. You don't got to piss on my idea, T.

TALISHA. Just cause you have the idea it a girl don't mean it is, Margie. Jesus. Sometimes you as dumb as you look.

(TALISHA *texts.*)

(MARGIE *is speechless for a moment.*)

(MARGIE *shifts her weight.*)

MARGIE. Okay. You seriously fucking all over my good news, T, which is like bullshit, right. You making me feel like that nurse did. How am I gonna do this if you ain't with me every step? Okay you lucky I gotta pee which is what you do when you PG but you seriously. Cause I don't know how I. And it is, it's bullshit. Just because that old dude beat you up –

(TALISHA *looks up from texting, finally revealing her face, one quarter of which is varying shades of black and blue and purple.*)

TALISHA. What? Say it again. Say it again.

(MARGIE *looks at* TALISHA.)

(TALISHA *looks at* MARGIE.)

(TALISHA *jumps at* MARGIE, *as if she might pounce on her.*)

(MARGIE *startles, then exits to go to the bathroom.*)

MARGIE. You just lucky I gotta pee. I'm just trying to figure out how all this baby stuff gonna work – .

(TALISHA *texts.*)

(MARGIE *is gone.*)

TALISHA. *(referring to the texting)* His sorry ass trying to make it up to me.

ANNIE. Does it hurt?

(TALISHA *texts, does not answer, as* ANNIE *waits.*)

ANNIE. It's…it's cause lately I been thinking a lot about. Maybe we.

(a text for TALISHA*)*

I been thinking about stuff like…like Shane Wilkes –

TALISHA. Ain't seen him since he went away for those cars. Who knew you get so much time just for stealing some crappy cars?

ANNIE. Remember those parties? In eighth grade when the girls would wear different lipstick and so at the end of them the boys could see how many colors they got going on their things by the end of the night?

TALISHA. Those were some good parties, yeah.

ANNIE. Well. I been thinking, maybe they. Really weren't. I been remembering. How with Shane. He expected more, he expected me to really do it but I like way chickened out. Just him asking me made me think if I drank a whole bottle of Palmolive wouldn't be enough to clean. Don't even want to talk up no guys cause you never know what they really…and lately everything happening so fast. One minute ladybug next minute foom, burnt –

TALISHA. Shane Wilkes wasn't even that cute. You ain't never had no sense, Anniegirl. You just went in there with the wrong kid, that's all.

(ANNIE *looks at* TALISHA *as* TALISHA *texts.*)

This new phone ten times better than what you and Margie got.

ANNIE. Maybe you should see a doctor something?

TALISHA. What d'you care? You don't care.

ANNIE. I do. You look like you really –

TALISHA. I look? You should see how *he* look. I dish it out, Annie.

ANNIE. He so nice about the phone, wonder what make him so mad later.

TALISHA. Older guys just like things certain ways is all. Like today he take me to the mall tell me pick whatever phone I like, right? I look in the case and my face get hot, right? I don't want to pick something too much, right? I point to one and he say naw, baby, who you think I am some kinda of chump? Pick again. This time I be sweatin' right? Like I can feel sweat dripping down the back my shirt, right? So I pick again. See he got all his boys with him and he don't want me make him look like he some broke ass scrub in front of them can't afford a nice phone. So he turn to one of them, and he say, she must think I'm a chump, shit. And his boy laugh loud right. And then all them start laughing loud and my guy started to get mad right, like real angry, and then he say, he say T who the hell you been with that make you feel you don't deserve the best, right? And one of his boys says well she ain't been with me yet, and I know I gotta answer right the next time and my guy says Now you look in that case baby girl and you tell me which you want. I so, I so don't want to get it wrong again so I look in and I pick this and he say that my baby girl. And I stop sweatin cause I did it right for him. The tones, the minutes, the apps is all unlimited I can pick all I want. You got Malik on a string like this?

(*TALISHA texts.*)

TALISHA. *(cont.)* Shane Wilkes: those were some good times, Annie. Those was much easier times than picking the right phone, shit.

ANNIE. Yeah....

(*TALISHA looks at ANNIE.*)

(*TALISHA stops texting.*)

(*TALISHA looks at ANNIE for a long time.*)

TALISHA. Margie too stupid to know you ain't even done it once yet.

ANNIE. Sure I done it.

TALISHA. I'll eat this phone if that true.

ANNIE. Could be true.

TALISHA. But it not.

ANNIE. ...it not.

TALISHA. We making you try to get a baby daddy one you ain't even had a first one yet.

ANNIE. The plan just seeming like it ain't the right thing, right? That nurse and the gloves, your guy and that phone. This guy seems seriously crazy, right? I mean look at your face –

(*ANNIE goes to touch TALISHA's face gently.*)

(*TALISHA almost lets her, then darts away.*)

TALISHA. Like what else I got to do?

ANNIE. Maybe there's more for us –

TALISHA. What that mean more? I don't give a crap about boats. What else the fuck I gonna – ? More: shit.

(*TALISHA texts.*)

It bad enough I gotta start from scratch cause after I got this phone, when we got back from the mall, he was all like why you show me up like that, T? Why you make me look like some kinda – . After all that, I started to you know bleed kinda, kinda like I thought my soul was bleeding out, I really think my soul – So I gotta start over with this baby stuff. But I can handle it. I keep my word.

(TALISHA texts.)

TALISHA. *(cont.)* 'Cause you and me could use a little baby love us all for us. Right about now. If you ask me. What else we got?

(TALISHA texts.)

Best thing about this phone is the keyboard so quick it keeps my hands busy. Sometimes they kinda shake, right – ? You know what we need is to get this shit organized.

ANNIE. What?

TALISHA. I'm gonna text my guy and see if he got a friend for you.

ANNIE. A friend? No, no –

TALISHA. Yeah, a real guy who really know what he doing, not some high school chump.

(TALISHA texts.)

If it was Margie I say no way. But you do fine with Mr. Picasso Tattoo over here, you do fine with one of these guys.

(a text for TALISHA)

BINGO, yo. My guy gonna hook you up good. Gave him your cell so he meet you anywhere. Krispy Kreme, park, anywhere, he'll be there and he get the job done right.

ANNIE. T –

TALISHA. T. You got it right: I knew we still friends. Right? Please don't let me be all alone, right? Annie? Please? You all I. Think I got.

(An empty street at night.)

(KEERA wears a white, very flowy, very virginal night-gown, a jacket over her shoulders. She also wears sneakers. Everything she wears is a bit threadbare.)

ANNIE. Cause I'm thinking I get my Aunt Rae to spring for some of them shoes, right?

KEERA. Huh?

ANNIE. A pair of them satin shoes like you talk about, right? She put up money for anything got to do with shopping.

KEERA. Slippers, right.

ANNIE. Maybe get my Dad to take me one of them dances. Cause I ain't like Margie, just thinking about sweaters and Coach, and I ain't like Talisha just sitting there, purple and blue all up and down…like it nothing, like having her hands shake is –

KEERA. Your text made it sound awful –

ANNIE. I'm sorry to wake you up, I didn't know who else would listen – . But you didn't have to meet me on the corner, I would have found your house okay.

KEERA. It's confusing. Tiny street and out of the way.

ANNIE. And why you out of breath?

KEERA. Glad you been keeping up with my texts, about those satin slippers, the pure hearts – Next we got to get you knowing your Bible. On Sunday, you come to church with me. There's that music. And cookies and juice right after. Pastor say the more youth I bring in to come to church, as a thank you he have me over his house for Sunday dinner.

ANNIE. I'm thinking you help me now, like you did with that radio, in the kitchen.

KEERA. His wife do the table up real nice over there. Table-cloth and nothing plastic on the table the whole meal.

ANNIE. Maybe you help me *now* though, not Sunday: *now.*

KEERA. If you come with me to church Pastor can help you and invite us *both* to dinner. You, me, the Pastor, his wife –

ANNIE. So you texting me to get a free meal.

KEERA. It ain't that it *free* it that it at the Pastor's–

ANNIE. What about all the food and games you been saying you got at your own house?

KEERA. I deserve a good meal.

ANNIE. And how come you meet me on the corner? How out the way could you live for real?

KEERA. My folks is particular – .

ANNIE. And thought you too good for sneakers like the rest of us.

KEERA. It's so late, I just threw everything on –

ANNIE. Why we meetin' on a corner, Keera? In the dark, in the middle of the night, in your nightgown, if your daddy dressin' you in ball gowns and you all play Yahtzee –

KEERA. You don't want to know about me.

ANNIE. What I want to know is the truth right?

KEERA. The truth. The truth is: every second of every day I pray to be someone else, anyone else, but me, for even just a moment. Eventhough I am good. I am, I am so. Good. I. Visit my father every week. Don't got no one to take me so I take the Greyhound. I go every week. Honor thy father and thy mother: that thy days may be long upon the land which the Lord thy God giveth thee. I go every week even though he got on that orange jump suit. And I got to talk to him behind glass through a phone I know he found his way. He the one, in his letters, start telling me about the Word. Start telling me to read my Bible. That when I started in going to church, after my daddy went away. My mom ain't never found her way. She plays the coin slots down Foxwoods. Takes her whole paycheck down Foxwoods. She don't remember my gym clothes. She barely remember what grade I'm on. But. Pastor say his home always open, long as my heart stay pure and I work for the Lord and that what my texts be doin'. I doing the work of the Lord. I deserve tablecloths and real forks and real spoons.

(beat)

I deserve them. I deserve them. I should be wearing satin, I should be shielded, I should be playing Yahtzee, I should, I should, I. I. *(a recovery:)* This is vanity, Keera. This is a sin, Keera, this is sin, Keera, this is sin, this is sin, this is –

(**KEERA** *bows her head.*)

(**MALIK** *in the clearing.*)

(*A shooting star.*)

(**MALIK** *watches it in the night sky.*)

(*The kitchen.*)

(**MYRNA** *and* **ANNIE**.)

MYRNA. Whole time he sittin there behind his desk talking
about rules, waving it around, like it a bad exam-
ple of something. He call me in in the day, I get all
dressed up, I think he gonna tell me that office want
to have me in do something aside of cleaning. I get all
dressed – . But exactly where it say I can't have a little
computer time? Those computers sit on all night: hun-
dreds of computers up in that place and how many
we got? How a person supposed to better themselves if
they ain't got good use of good things? Huh? Should
have double checked it was in my bag, should have
triple – . I knew that girl was bad luck, probably cast
some churchy spell up on me.

ANNIE. You find another job.

MYRNA. Right, who needs a job like that anyway? Don't do
no thinking on a job like that. What I needs a job that
lets me use my mind, that wants my opinion on things.

ANNIE. Maybe we all eat dinner together tonight? Since you
home. You change those clothes then we eat dinner,
play checkers, take your mind off –

MYRNA. I just said I want my mind *on*: look for a better
job. And this my special outfit. Ain't nothing wrong
with my special outfit. Least I put it to good use. Took
myself out. Celebrated being rid of that goddamn
place. Mind on. That's the future, Anniegirl.

ANNIE. You ask what I want for my birthday, that what
want –

MYRNA. I don't got time to be thinking on some cake and
candles.

ANNIE. I didn't say cake or candles.

MYRNA. No, no this the worst time have your Aunt Rae up in here for any kind of party. Stuff like this never happen to your Aunt Rae and she let you know it. She'll bring over her Mary Kay and have me done up like Bozo the Clown, send me out looking for who's hiring. Your Aunt Rae get all up in my business and it take three glasses of punch get her out again. How they *fire* me over some lousy *computer*? Naw, if you so into dinner you go into the cabinet and bring down the crocker your own self.

ANNIE. ...It's...It's called a Crock. Pot.

MYRNA. ...That's what I said.

ANNIE. It's definitely *not* called a crocker.

MYRNA. Who cares what it called, I said I don't want people up in here.

(MYRNA *begins to busy herself in the kitchen.*)

ANNIE. I'd think if you a writer and all, you know that, you want to use the right words. You can't cook a nice family dinner with checkers in a crocker cause it don't exist. I don' know why you so surprised they fire you. I told you stay out of those people's office things. You say you got words in you but you don't even listen. What kind of mother don't want to eat with her own kids? Of course they fire you, you can't even put a sentence together. You shouldn't've been writing there you should've been cleaning there. That's what you do: you *clean:* other people's crap in other people's lives when you should be listening, you should be paying *attention*, to me. Instead you watching what other people throwing away, what other people with real houses and real jobs and real whole lives're not using, what, all because one teacher back in the sixth grade told you you wrote one story that was good –

MYRNA. And who told *you* you so goddamn special?

ANNIE. Who the one stupid enough to get knocked up before the end of junior high school – All my life you treating me like I you. You punishing me like I you. Those stories don't make no kinda – . ' Can't even keep my books in here, you touch all over them, try to get all in them, when you can't barely read one word – . I'm trying to –

MYRNA. Trying to what?

ANNIE. Say maybe there's a different –

MYRNA. Different? You ain't different from me and you sure as hell ain't better, I can tell you that.

ANNIE. It's that I got this burn –

MYRNA. This world will spit you out. Chew you up, spit you out –

ANNIE. I'm sayin I think maybe, for me, there's more than –

MYRNA. More than what? You think you better than me?

ANNIE. I ain't talking about you, I ain't said –

MYRNA. Whole world crack open for you like an egg cause you deserve better than me? You don't deserve better than me. Ain't no one up in here thinking you so special you deserve better, Annemarie Desmond. Cause I'll tell you the truth, the honest truth, you ain't worth shit.

(Lights rise on the tattoo parlor.)

(ANTWOINE works, draws, looks up to see ANNIE.)

ANNIE. Bigger. For real.

ANTWOINE. Sweet sixteen.

ANNIE. Down to my toes, up to my neck. Maybe them flames could even lick up to my eyes even. Can you do that, up to my eyes like that?

ANTWOINE. Can't make that no bigger, girl, my cousin already pissed there ain't hardly any red left up in here.

ANNIE. Whatever, right? Just do the damn thing, right?

(ANTWOINE looks at ANNIE.)

ANTWOINE. Sure you shouldn't be home in bed sleeping tight?

(ANNIE *indicates* ANTWOINE'*s work.*)

ANNIE. *(Abrupt. Frantic change of subject. Searching:)* You always knew you wanted to draw?

ANTWOINE. You should be home. Covers pulled up.

ANNIE. Like when you was little? Like someone liked what you drew and said you're good, you on the right path with that.

ANTWOINE. Used to draw little cartoons for my Dad. Corny, but he he liked them –

ANNIE. Cause it'd much be easier around here if I had something I was really good at, something lift me up above everything else everybody else. Like this girl down the hall in my building she plays the cello and got into one of those programs. She goes to high school in New Hampshire now. Comes home at Christmas only cause they lock the dorm. That her ticket out and she not letting go of that ticket for nothing. I don't have a ticket.

ANTWOINE. What can I do for you, Sweet Sixteen. Can't tell me no one waiting on you at home.

ANNIE. It's Annie. And no one waiting for me at home.

ANTWOINE. It's real late.

(a text for ANNIE*)*

(a text for ANNIE*)*

(a text for ANNIE*)*

ANNIE. Stupid phone. Could text all night, I'd still feel all alo –

(She turns off the phone.)

The only calls I got on my birthday, that night I got my tattoo, some punk ass boy don't really got a ticket either. Think he does. But he stuck like the rest of us. Well, not you. You draw. That could take you out of here –

ANTWOINE. I talk too much. I…I get distracted.

ANNIE. You can move people, change people. Like you said.

ANTWOINE. That guy with the ship? That. Dude asked for a boat, small boat, I. I'd been practicing but. My fingers were nervous. Heart was racing. Wanted to show what I thought I could do but I got carried. Away. Cause I thought, this cat need more than a boat. This cat need to see the ocean, this cat need to ride them waves and my hands wouldn't stop, my hands….Cousin still let me in at nights, but can't let me get set up for real. Blood on the chair, down to the floor. My waves tore his skin up into a storm. Took my cousin three weeks make it look like something again. I did good on you, I think. I get distracted, too many thoughts when I. Work. My cousin say people don't want a mouth of thoughts comin' at em –

ANNIE. Your cousin's all wrong. I love what you say.

ANTWOINE. Yeah?

ANNIE. I like what you drew on me.

ANTWOINE. I had a beautiful canvas.

(ANNIE *smiles.*)

Beautiful canvas, beautiful picture.

ANNIE. Fire.

ANTWOINE. Fire, cause you don't choose the tattoo, the tattoo chooses you.

ANNIE. Talisha chose my tattoo.

ANTWOINE. Little piece of you chose it too. You got fire and maybe that's a good thing. All by itself. Maybe you don't need a ticket, beautiful as you is.

(ANNIE *blushes.*)

It's true. No one tell you that before? That you something special?

ANNIE. …nope.

ANTWOINE. I can't be the first person tell you you something. Anyone'd be stupid not to want to feel that type of fire –

(ANNIE *opens her shirt, revealing a large red, flame tattoo.*)

It's late. Maybe you should –

ANNIE. Nobody waiting on me at home.

ANTWOINE. I probably should get back to – . I can't be somebody's boyfriend, right. I ain't that kind of –

ANNIE. Maybe we burn right up together maybe.

ANTWOINE. You understand what I'm saying? Right?

ANNIE. Down to our toes. Up to our necks.

ANTWOINE. Burn up...Yeah I, I could – . Cause it not like we...Cause what else...what else we got, better to do than feel special, for a minute, right? Tonight, tomorrow, next week, next year. What the hell else we got?

ANNIE. Blue.

ANTWOINE. Blue.

ANNIE. Red.

ANTWOINE. Red.

ANNIE. *Foom.*

ANTWOINE. Foom.

(ANNIE *kisses* ANTWOINE.)

(ANTWOINE *begins to remove* ANNIE*'s clothing.*)

(*They kiss. They do more than kiss.*)

(*The sound of a large fire burning until we hear the sound of wind.*)

(*Wind howls. It is a warm wind. More like the Santa Ana Foehn wind, even though those do not happen in the east.*)

(*The clearing.*)

(MALIK. *A bit older. He wears dress pants and shirt, nice shoes.*)

(ANNIE *sits in the clearing. She appears older, too.*)

(*A gift box sits nearby.*)

ANNIE. Well open it. Go on.

MALIK. You shouldn't a gotten me anything.

(MALIK *opens the box and lifts out the telescope, put back together with duct tape.*)

ANNIE. I know the University of Iowa probably got its own telescopes –

MALIK. Naw, naw, thank you.

ANNIE. But thought you might appreciate having this one back.

MALIK. Yeah, yeah, of course, yeah.

ANNIE. Thanks for meeting me. It been so long. Was worried you so mad you might not want to meet –

MALIK. Senior year just took off, right? Ain't barely had no time for nothin'.

ANNIE. Right.

MALIK. You keep up with Talisha and them?

ANNIE. Nah. Barely see anyone no more: T gone an dropped out, moved in with that old guy. Margie in night school since she had the baby. She do her apartment real cute. She and Jerome only on the list two months and public housing got them a spot. And Keera, she transferred to Saint Joseph's.

MALIK. So you really like my speech?

ANNIE. Sure.

MALIK. That don't sound like you think it great, maybe just good.

ANNIE. The stuff about the clear blue horizon that's ours to touch and all that? I loved that. Really. Your moms must be proud.

MALIK. I hope she be alright.

ANNIE. She be alright. Too much pride in you for her to get sick again.

MALIK. Hope.

ANNIE. Dr. Fitzgerald be proud, too.

MALIK. She didn't even make it to February vacation. The good teachers always leave.

ANNIE. The good teachers always run out.

MALIK. Could stay if they really wanted. Forget about the children they should leave one or two teachers behind, teach Johnny to read and write and add before he gets into trouble.

(**MALIK** *and* **ANNIE***'s eyes meet.*)

She should have stayed, alls I mean. Don't you think she should have stayed?

(pause)

Do you want to come to my party?

ANNIE. Nah. Told my moms I be home by eight. Sucks. But if I'm not she lock the dead bolt on me now. Used to be only time me and her talked was before school. Ladybug. Now she can barely say my name, nevermind call me something special. Your house is on fire: your children will – . Can't even get her to look at me now –

MALIK. Well, invitation open.

(**ANNIE** *looks at* **MALIK.***)*

This a nice present.

ANNIE. I aim to please, Malik.

MALIK. But I think you should keep it. Use it.

ANNIE. ...sure, okay. Thank you. For everything. The stuff you said back in September. Anyway. Christmas we can come up here, take a look, talk.

MALIK. I'll be home before Christmas.

ANNIE. Maybe.

MALIK. Shoot, we got all summer.

ANNIE. I don't.

MALIK. Right.

ANNIE. That's cool, you're gonna leave it.

MALIK. Sure.

ANNIE. I want to check on those faces, right. If they looking down at me laughing, thinking we all just some stupid wasted joke around here, I want to be able to look right back at them. Meet they gaze.

MALIK. You should look up. Higher than those faces. Higher than those planes.

(As **MALIK** *takes the tripod out of the box, sets up the telescope.)*

Well I'll leave this up, don't worry. You see me way more than at Christmas, you see. I should. My mom don't want me gone too long.

*(***MALIK** *goes to* **ANNIE**, *kisses her demurely on the forehead.)*

Stay sweet, Anniegirl.

ANNIE. There was one thing about your speech. Like if it was *me* giving your speech. I'd. Say something about that box of milk, like sugar, on your cabinet shelves. We supposed to be drinking real milk 'stead we fed that powdered kind that looks like sugar – school feeds us sugar, the streets of this place feed us sugar – and we like it, we lap it up, we at the ready for it like it Vitamin D added, one hundred percent pure goodness meant to feed us stead of rot our insides out. Milk like sugar on all our shelves in this place and we happy for it. Shit. Stupid.

MALIK. Not so stupid.

*(***MALIK** *smiles, exits.)*

*(***ANNIE** *breathes out, a less than light sigh.)*

(She stands, reveals a very pregnant profile.)

(She goes to the telescope, looks in.)

(She scans the audience: left, right.)

(She raises the telescope, slowly, slowly.)

(She steps back. She smiles.)

(She looks into the telescope.)

(She scans the sky: left, right, middle.)

(She exhales.)

(Darkness.)

End of Play